Holiness

A Guide for Beginners

∞

Also available from Sophia Institute Press®
by Dom Hubert van Zeller:

Holiness for Housewives
(and Other Working Women)

Dom Hubert van Zeller

Holiness
A Guide for Beginners

∞

Formerly entitled:
Sanctity in Other Words

SOPHIA INSTITUTE PRESS®

Manchester, New Hampshire

Holiness: A Guide for Beginners was first published in the United States in 1963 under the title *Sanctity in Other Words* by Templegate Publishers, Springfield, Illinois.

Copyright © 1997 Sophia Institute Press®
Printed in the United States of America
All rights reserved
Jacket design by Joan Barger

The cover painting is a detail from *The Annunciation* by Fra Angelico, in the Museum of San Marco, Florence, Italy (Nimatallah/Art Resource, New York).

Sophia Institute Press®
Box 5284, Manchester, NH 03108
1-800-888-9344

Nihil Obstat: Ralph Russell, O.S.B., *Censor Deputatus*
Imprimatur: B. C. Butler, *Abb. Praes.*
September 8, 1962

Library of Congress Cataloging-in-Publication Data

Van Zeller, Hubert, 1905-
    [Sanctity in other words]
    Holiness : a guide for beginners / Hubert van Zeller.
      p.   cm.
    Originally published : Sanctity in other words. Springfield, Ill. :
    Templegate Publishers, 1963.
    ISBN 0-918477-54-9 (hdbk. : alk. paper)
    ISBN 0-918477-45-X (pbk. : alk. paper)
    1. Spiritual life — Catholic Church. 2. Sanctification. 3. Holiness —
    Christianity. 4. Catholic Church — Doctrines. I. Title.
BX2350.2.V1934   1997
234'.8 — dc20   96-42443 CIP

97 98 99 00 01 10 9 8 7 6 5 4 3 2

Contents

Editor's Note: The biblical references in the following pages are based on the Douay-Rheims edition of the Old and New Testaments. Quotations from the Psalms and some of the historical books of the Bible have been cross-referenced with the differing names and enumeration in the Revised Standard Version, using the following symbol: (RSV =).

Holiness
A Guide for Beginners

∞

Chapter 1

What Holiness Is and Is Not

∞

If personal holiness is thought of as being a name at the top of a list, it is understood wrong. If it is thought of as something that merits a feast in the Church's calendar, it is understood wrong. If it is thought of as something to which is attached the power of working miracles, it is understood wrong. If it is thought of as mooning about in a state of pious contentment (or sweet ecstasy or noble and aloof virtue), it is understood wrong. There is nothing "superior" — in the sense of being one up on everybody else — about it.

The way to think of sanctity is as something that, by being generous and faithful to grace, gives back to God the love He has given to the soul. So it is for God's sake, more than for our own, that we should want to be saints. We work away at holiness not because we are ambitious, and want to be experts in a particular kind of lofty career, but because God wants us to be saints and is praised by our striving after sanctity.

Holiness

Anyone can be holy, or rather *act* holy, so long as others are saying, "There's a saint for you," but sooner or later this sort of holiness wears off. Either the person sees the trap, becomes humble, and goes ahead toward real holiness, or keeping up the act becomes too much of a strain and there's a swing toward worldliness and perhaps to a lasting unholiness. The whole secret of sanctity is that it is a thing of grace, and so cannot be switched on as a part to be played.

This means that however determined you are to be a saint, you will not become one if you rely on your own strength of mind. The only thing that can get you to sanctity is God's grace. You will need all the strength of mind you have just to work together with God's grace, but if you imagine that making good, strong resolutions will carry you the whole way, you are wrong. About the first thing to happen will be that God lets you break some of those good, strong resolutions before you get properly started. This will be to put you in your place, and show you that you can do nothing without Him.

Once you are decently humbled, knowing that left to yourself you cannot even carry out the things that you very much want to carry out, you are getting ready to be used. You are being softened up like a steak. When all

6

the toughness and pride and glamorized ideas of holiness have been beaten out of you by the down-to-earth action of truth, then God has got something there on which He can work. Without false notions and fancy plans, you can now begin to fall in with the true notions of holiness and with the plan God has in mind for you.

It stands to reason. God is not going to reward anyone else's work but His own. You cannot expect Him to recognize a holiness that He has done nothing to bring about. When you get right down to it, there is only one real goodness, one perfection, one sanctity, and that is God's. When man invents a holiness of his own, God lets him look for it but does not help him find it, because a holiness of one's own does not exist, and it is a waste of time searching for it. It is as if someone were to look for moonlight without the moon. Once you admit that all moonlight is bound to come from one particular place, and that it is a thing you cannot make yourself, you have learned something.

∞

Another thing to notice right at the beginning about holiness is that there is no cut-and-dried pattern about it. It is what God wants out of you, and because you are not exactly the same as anyone else, the holiness that is to be yours will not be exactly like anyone else's. The model of all holiness is our Lord, and unless you grow to be like Him, you will never get anywhere in holiness, but this does not mean that all who follow Him will end up exactly alike. Our Lord appeals to us in His way, and we answer Him in our way.

If twenty artists are told to paint a picture of the Crucifixion, they will all show the same thing but in twenty different ways. There will be twenty quite separate pictures, no two alike. This is how God wants our response to be: each one his own. Now, just as it would show a weakness in one of those twenty artists to copy as closely as possible the painting of the artist next to him, so it would be a weakness for one follower of our Lord to copy as closely as possible the particular holiness of another follower. He should make it his first job to follow our Lord. The ways by which others have followed our Lord can be a tremendous help, just as the ways other people paint can be a tremendous help to painting, but our Lord, who is Himself "the way, the truth, and the life,"[1] wants something out of you that is

[1] John 14:6.

your own to give and is not just a copy. The saints produce masterpieces because of each one's likeness to our Lord, not because of each one's likeness to another. By all means, let us imitate the way in which the saints went about it, but by no means let us copy the results. God wants an original reproduction of Himself, not a forgery.

All right then, what is it that the saints do that makes them into saints? The answer is that they do two things: on the one side they keep clear of anything that they think is going to get in the way of grace, and on the other they head directly for our Lord. The only thing to be added to this is that they do it for the glory of God and not for what they can get out of it. They are the ones who "seek first the kingdom of God," and for the King's sake rather than for their own, and who are ready to wait as long as God likes for the day when "all these things" shall be added to them.[2]

So it is not that the saints do particularly "saintly" things (like fierce penances, whole nights spent on their knees, miracles, prophecies, or raptures in prayer); it is more that they do all things in a particularly saintly way,

[2] Matt. 6:33.

9

in exactly the way that they feel God wants. To them the only thing in the world that matters is God's will. They know that by doing God's will as perfectly as they can, they are imitating our Lord, they are expressing charity, and they are being true to the best that is in them.

All this should be a great encouragement to us because it shows that our service of God does not depend upon how we feel about it, but upon how God looks at it; not upon acts that are seen to be heroic, but upon how ready we are to let God draw heroism out of us; not upon battling our way to a certain point that will give us the title of "saint," but upon following blindly the course that is set by God's will.

Chapter 2

What Holiness Does

You will see from what has just been said that sanctity, like everything else in life, should be looked at from God's point of view rather than from man's. We have come from God and we exist for Him; our holiness must come from God and must exist for Him. We believe that the purpose of man, of life, of creation, of everything, is the glory of God. Does this mean anything to us? What is *glory* anyway?

St. Augustine says that glory is "clear knowledge joined to praise" — which actually tells us more than just what glory is because it shows what we have to do about it. It shows how we give glory. Praise of God in prayer gives glory; service of one another in charity gives glory; desire to follow our Lord gives glory; willingness to do God's will gives glory. So the whole point of sanctity, then, is that it gives glory to God.

Our Lord, who is sanctity itself, shows us how while He was on earth He gave glory to the Father. "I have glorified You on earth; I have finished the work which

You gave me to do."[3] What was that "work"? Quite simply it was the Father's will. This, of course, meant doing a lot of particular things — such as preaching, working miracles, founding a Church, suffering the Passion — but all was summed up in faithfully fulfilling the Father's will. When, right at the end, He said from the Cross, "It is finished,"[4] our Lord did not only mean that His life was finished, but that the work the Father had given Him to do, the task of fulfilling the divine will, was now completely rounded off and that there was nothing more to be done.

In being "obedient unto death"[5] to the Father's will, our Lord was giving us a lesson in glory. It was the day-to-day obedience in things not noticed by anyone except His mother and the closest of His friends that gave glory to the Father just as much as the miracles, prayers, and teaching gave glory. Now, if our chief duty as Christians is to be reliving our Lord's life in our own world, then it is not going to be in performing the great works of Christ but in performing the little ones. And

[3] John 17:4.
[4] John 19:30.
[5] Phil. 2:8.

just as the little works He did were not little in the eyes of the Father because they were being done perfectly by the Son, so the little ones we do are not little to the Father because we are trying to do them perfectly with the Son.

A quite ordinary duty, such as writing a letter of thanks or getting up at the right time in the morning, can give great glory to God. It is answering to His will. The ordinariness of the actual job is raised so that it shares in the obedience of Christ. From the tip of the pen (if we are writing that letter), glory is flowing out to God; from the effort to throw off the sheets (if it is that duty of getting up), there is an immediate output of glory to God. At every instant of the day, doing what we have to do because God wills us to do it, we are handling glory.

Breathing the air of God's glory, we only have to breathe it in His direction and we are there. As the fish swimming in the sea and the birds flying in the sky, we are moving about in what might be called "glory-space." It is not as though we had to get onto another planet to find sanctity and give glory to God, or even alter the position we are in on this one (provided that we are where God wants us to be), because God's presence is everywhere and all we have to do is to live in it and praise Him in it.

God is glorified in all His creation, and not only in human beings who can use their minds to speak His praises. Nature praises Him because it gets its existence from Him and works according to His laws. It is fairly easy to see how God is glorified by sunsets and roses and snow-capped mountains, because these things reflect something of divine beauty, but He is also glorified by dull things like stones and cabbage and rain. Moving one step higher, we find little difficulty in seeing God glorified in puppies and small chickens and friendly polar bears at the zoo, because these things are lovable and nice, but He is also glorified by snakes and toads and rats. Each separate piece of God's creation, by existing in the kind of existence God means it to have, gives glory to God.

This idea of everything having on it the glow of God's look — like the warmth of the sun showing in a haze of heat over the water — seems clear enough when we take the trouble to think about it. To the saints, such a view of creation is a settled state of mind. Outward objects are seen and loved as being reflections of Him who made them. That is why St. Paul said that the visible things were there to draw our minds to a knowledge of the invisible Creator.[6] That is why St. Francis of Assisi called natural things, like the sky and the sun, by the title of "brother" and "sister." They were all in the family. They all bore on them the Father's likeness.

You can imagine what a difference it would make to your life if you saw all around you signposts pointing to the presence of God. Not only would nature and human beings proclaim the glory of God, but even in the ordinary happenings from hour to hour and from day to day you would welcome God's will. You would be drawn at once to show gratitude for the pleasant things that happened, knowing that God had provided them, and the unpleasant ones you would accept as part of your share in the Passion. So it would mean that you could live out your life under what St. Augustine described as the canopy or firmament of God's will.

So that is what sanctity does. First it glorifies God, from whom all sanctity comes. And second it discovers more and more material with which to express this

[6] Cf. Rom. 1:20.

glory. Where the ordinary Sunday-Mass-and-nothing-more kind of Catholic sees the service of God as a tiresome duty to be gotten through somehow, the saint sees the service of God as a marvelous opportunity. To the one there seem to be few signs of God's love in a world of muddle and unfairness; to the other there are signs of His love on every side, even in confusion and disappointment. To the one there are just people, nice ones and nasty ones; to the other there are souls, all of them somehow lovable and all of them reflecting the love of God. To the one there are earthly needs and trials to worry about; to the other there is nothing to worry about because earthly needs and trials are handed over to God. The one dreads lots of things as evil; the other dreads only one evil — sin.

Chapter 3

Holiness and Happiness

L ooking at the title of this chapter, you must be careful not to make the mistake of asking yourself first whether you are saintly and second whether you are happy. Both are stupid questions, getting you nowhere. It is only sham saints who are forever wondering how holy they are; the real ones forget about themselves in their desire to please God. In the same way, it is only people who are not awfully happy who question their happiness. So take whatever is coming in this chapter not as something personal, meaning *you*, but more as something that will show you the general direction in which both holiness and happiness are to be found.

Have you ever noticed how the holiest people you have come across always seem to be the happiest? You would think that enclosed nuns in their Carmelite con-vents, with no possessions and no pleasures such as movies and parties, might be lonely and sad. But not at all: they are just the ones who seem to be laughing whenever you visit them. Then on the other side of it, you would think that men and women who have lots of money and lovely houses would be proclaiming their happiness all day long. But it does not work out like this. The lonely ones are men with two or three wives ("which ought to be company enough," you would have said) and the women who are so busy running after pleasure that they are never alone.

It is a known fact that the people who kill themselves are mostly the rich and the worldly, not the poor and the religious. Does not this prove something? Well, it points to a lot of things, but chiefly it seems to show that filling your life with enjoyment only empties your life of happiness, and that collecting more and more money or possessions or power simply does not work.

After what our Lord has said, this is only to be expected. "A man's life does not consist in the abundance of his possessions."[7] "Seek first the kingdom of God."[8] "Your treasure is in Heaven where the rust does not consume and thieves do not break through and

[7] Luke 12:15.
[8] Matt. 6:33.

steal."[9] "What does it profit a man if he gain the whole world and suffer the loss of his own soul?"[10] "The peace which I give is not the peace which the world gives, for my peace no man can take from you."[11] Remember the parable of Dives and Lazarus,[12] the parable of the rich man who tried to store up his goods in bigger and bigger barns,[13] and the parable of the woman who gave away even the last of her savings.[14] Remember the incident of the rich young man who was called to be a disciple, but who turned away because he could not bring himself to part from his wealth.[15]

Remember that our Lord promised that those who carried their burdens willingly, with Him and as though they were His, would find the weight light; the hard yoke of service would turn into something sweet. "Come to me, all you who are heavy laden," He invited. He

---

[9] Cf. Matt. 6:20.
[10] Mark 8:36.
[11] Cf. John 14:27; John 16:22.
[12] Luke 16:19-31.
[13] Luke 12:16-21.
[14] Mark 12:41-44.
[15] Mark 10:17-22.

would ease matters for these hard-pressed souls, and they would find rest for their souls and peace.[16]

The strange thing is that worldly people, quite sinful people, read these words of our Lord and do not deny them. They know in their hearts that what He said was perfectly true. They admit the uselessness of luxury when it comes to the question of happiness, and they know that hardship cannot on its own make people miserable. But they cannot bring themselves to put the gospel teaching into practice. They are afraid to let go of their pleasures, and they are afraid of the Cross. Sanctity would be their one solution, but they do not want to think about what might be expected of them if they went all out for it.

If even worldly people can understand the worthlessness of a happiness that rests on pleasure and possessions, you may be sure that philosophers agree about it, too. The wise men of China, India, and Greece all told the same story: do not put your trust in what can only be toys and passing amusements. The Greeks — Socrates and Plato especially — made a science of this particular point, and it might be a good thing to take a look at

[16] Matt. 11:28-30.

what they decided about it. (If it bores you, skip it; the rest of this book is not going to be about the Greeks and their idea of happiness, so you will not be missing much if you do.) The philosophers of ancient civilization (before the coming of our Lord) explained how human beings could not help chasing after their own happiness. They said that man could arrive at happiness only if the good he was looking for was a real one. Man can never be happy, they said, in the enjoyment of a good that pretends to be a good but is not one really. They also laid down that every being seeks its own proper perfection. (The cabbage works at being the perfect cabbage; the growing caterpillar strains to become the perfect caterpillar so that it can become the perfect moth; the baby is all the time pressing on into youth, and the young are doing their best to model themselves according to a pattern they have set up for themselves as perfection.)

Now we can leave the Greeks and can bring in St. Thomas Aquinas, the Doctor of the Church who said that our human happiness "lies in the perfection of our highest faculties." This gets us one stage further, showing us that happiness and holiness go together. The highest faculties can find perfection only in the highest good — namely, God. So the highest happiness of man lies in drawing near to the perfect holiness of God. Now, from the point of view of this book, which is all about our sanctification, the important thing here is that God pours out His holiness to those who make His honor and glory their highest happiness.

So if we really mean to place our happiness in doing God's will, we cannot fail to grow in holiness. The argument goes around and around in what might be called a virtuous circle: we want happiness (see the philosophers), we look for it in God (see the saints), we set our highest faculties to work (see the theologians), we do God's will (see the saints again), and when we do this as well as we can, we become holy. And what about becoming happy, too? Yes, but happiness is a by-product. "Seek first the kingdom of God, and all these things" — happiness among them — "will be added to you."

Look at the life of St. Francis, and see how his story bears out the cycle (the various stages of the argument that come around to the beginning). He hungered for God, lived for God alone, made God's will his one aim, and at the end of his life — although blind, in pain, poor, and with his work apparently coming to nothing — proclaimed his overwhelming happiness. He knew the theory, and proved it.

Chapter 4

The Saints and Holiness

If St. Francis is a typical example of how sanctity works in the soul, he can be chosen to illustrate the various other sides of grace that are to be dealt with under the above heading. You would find roughly the same sort of thing showing up in the life of every saint: the willingness for anything that God may send, the desire to follow Christ in all things, the love that leaves self out of the picture and finds peace in doing so.

What many of us remember particularly about St. Francis is the way in which he kissed the leper's sores. What we must forget about it is that it was dramatic; what we must realize about it is that it was done to Christ. And this serves as a pretty good symbol of the saint's — of any saint's — approach to sanctity. Whatever is done in the way of charity to neighbors, whatever is endured in the way of mortification, whatever is taken in one's stride in the way of either work or pleasure is directed toward our Lord and united with His own action while He lived here on earth.

Holiness

The program is universal: nothing is left out of the Providence of God, and all is given back with as perfect a union of wills as possible. You can see at once from this how true holiness does not depend upon the extraordinary, but upon the ordinary, how it is an attitude of mind and not a list of holy achievements. Our mistake is always to judge a man's action by its success or failure, by whether or not the man has carried out what he set himself to do. God goes deeper than this and judges by the motive, the fidelity with which the desire has been kept up, and the degree of the soul's dependence upon His grace.

When you read the life of a saint, you are probably more impressed by the mortifications than by the motives, by the performance than by the perseverance, and by the sensation caused than by the submission given. If this is so, you have got it all wrong. The qualities to look for in a saint's life are the not-very-obvious ones, or at any rate not-very-popular ones: humility and charity. Exciting penances are fine (so long as God wants them), but they are hardly ever the reason why a person becomes a saint, hardly ever the final sign that a person *has* become a saint. The reasons and signs will be looked at more closely in a later chapter. At the moment, we are considering the habit of holiness as a state of mind rather than the causes and proofs of holiness as something to be canonized by the Church.

Suppose that you have a prisoner in a cell, condemned to a life sentence. Compare him to a hermit, a religious man who has bound himself by vow to the enclosure of his hut. The prisoner's state of mind is resentful, rebellious, unhappy; he is forever either planning to escape or hoping that his term of imprisonment may be shortened. The hermit's state of mind is quite different; he has taken on that kind of life and is trying to lead it as perfectly as he can; he has no thought of escape or of shortening the time he has dedicated to God. The life of the hermit is probably harder on the body than the prisoner's, and the hermit has to care entirely for himself. But does this make him less happy than the prisoner? Of course not. The hermit is doing everything for God, and is depending upon God. The prisoner is doing nothing for God, and is depending on himself and on the state. The hermit has made love his whole life, and welcomes every chance of showing love to God and to any stray visitor who may come along — to all the world. The prisoner wants only to get even with the people who have put him where he is, with his warders, with the whole world. Do you see the argument? Where the state of mind is right, everything else follows; where it is wrong, nothing brings relief or does any good.

The saints could take the hardships of penance and the disappointments of failure in their stride because there was only one thing that mattered for them — God's will. Since their state of mind was a continuous state of love, nothing could crush them except the sense of sin. And even the sense of sin could be endured where there was complete trust in the mercy of God. To be able to say, "Thy kingdom come, Thy will be done on earth as it is in Heaven"[17] *whatever happens* is to have found the secret of both holiness and peace of mind.

Now perhaps you can see how the really important part about the saints and sanctity is not a lot of fierce mortifications or a lot of wonderful visions. The really important part is giving oneself to God — surrendering and staying surrendered. The fierce penances are taken up by the saints to show God that soft living is not what they want, that a share in the sufferings of Christ is what they want, and that they want to help the world

[17] Matt. 6:10.

by making up for man's sins. Love and atonement are at the back of those fastings and scourgings. It was not that by fasting and scourging themselves the saints thought they could crash their way to sanctity; it was rather that they felt uncomfortable trying to follow our Lord by any but the hard way.

When St. Catherine of Siena was offered by our Lord the choice between the crown of roses and the crown of thorns, she chose at once the crown of thorns. She would not have committed the least sin by choosing the roses — our Lord had said that she could take which-ever she liked — but she knew that the thorns brought her nearer to Christ. She did not say, "Roses are worldly, and I renounce them as a sinful indulgence"; she said, "Roses are lovely, but I would feel silly wearing them when my Lord chose thorns." The good things of God's creation are put aside by the saints not because they are seen as evil all of a sudden, but because the absolute goodness of God is wanted more. It is like the child putting aside a toy when his mother comes in after being away. The greater love makes the love of lesser things fade out.

So when you read of the penances of the saints, be sure to keep these things in their right place. Holiness

Holiness

asks, as we shall see, for a lot of renunciation. But with the renunciations go many graces. Those who leave possessions, lands, houses, and families "for my name's sake," receive their hundredfold,[18] which must make the renunciation feel far less terrible. If we take up the Cross with Christ, bearing it with Him, then we come to know how truly His promises are fulfilled: the burden becomes light and the yoke sweet. But probably it is only the saints who can tell us this from their experience. If the burden weighs us down so that we long to be rid of it, and if the yoke embitters instead of sweetens, we have to admit that ours is not yet the state of mind to lay claim to holiness.

[18]Cf. Matt. 19:29.

Chapter 5

What Holiness Asks For

These three chapters (this one and the next two) are meant to pair off with the three theological virtues: faith, hope, and charity. Faith is what sanctity first of all demands of us; hope is what it leads to; charity is its foundation. If fidelity to the theological virtues makes up the duty of all who call themselves Christians, then the *perfection* of the theological virtues makes up the sanctity of those whom the Church calls saints. Holiness is not finding new virtues to practice that the ordinary Christian does not know about; it is going deeper into the old virtues that are the ordinary expression of Christianity.

In the same way, sanctity is not making more and more resolutions, collecting more and more pieties, or inventing more and more means of denying yourself. It is reliving the life of our Lord more and more by faith, hope, and charity. This simplifies the program a good deal, and if you think of holiness in any other way — particularly as multiplying acts of holiness — you not only think of it wrong, but you also add to the difficulties of arriving at it.

St. Paul says (quoting the prophet Habakkuk, incidentally, although he does not mention it) that "the just man lives by faith."[19] Now, if this is true of the just man, it is certainly true of the saint. Faith is precisely what the exceedingly just man lives by. In the light of faith, and *only* in the light that faith brings, the saint sees the truth about mankind. He sees why God created human beings who He knew would let Him down. He sees how God's love for these weak human beings is in no way contradicted by His allowing them to suffer. He sees that there is a reason behind temptation and war and insecurity — behind all the things people find so hard to square with their idea of God.

In other words, what God asks of His servants, what sanctity absolutely demands, is that kind of faith that looks beyond the outward appearance for a reality and truth that a worldly view denies. Reality, truth — the world, which is most of the time concerned with unreality and untruth, never stops trying to force its ideas upon the believing soul. The believing soul has to put

[19]Hab. 2:4; Rom. 1:17; Gal. 3:11.

up a barrier of unbreakable faith, or the unreal will lead the appetites astray and the untrue will lead the mind astray. We have probably often felt this. We have noticed how things that we know are not worthwhile can take up all of our interest and can absorb our whole desire. We have seen how things that we know to be false can be counted as true when we once begin to deceive ourselves.

The trouble is that if we go on feeding our appetites on ice cream and chocolates, the time will come when we will no longer feel interested in proper food. Even when we take the proper food that is given to us, we now no longer get any good from it. We have been nourished for too long on falsehood to know the meaning of truth. If this is what happens to those who slide into the ways of the world, how can we make sure that we keep our faces firmly fixed toward God and sanctity, reality and truth?

It has been pointed out on an earlier page how, in order to go to God, we must reflect God, and how, in order to be holy, we must allow God's own holiness to work itself out in us. In much the same way, in order to see reality and truth, we must have something in us of God's reality and truth. "They that worship the Father," says our Lord, "must worship in spirit and in truth."[20] We must be real people, as God is a real God; we must be true as God is true. All the pull is the other way: the world wants us to be sham people, false and shallow.

By faith we come to have a deeper understanding of what truth really means. It is something much more than just not-a-lie, not-a-heresy, not-a-hypocrisy. The saints were true in the sense of being what God meant them to be. And because they were true, they could see the world about them as it really is, as it is in God's sight. Truth is not only something we can see (like a watch telling "true" time or a set of scales giving a "true" balance), but is something we see *by*. In the light of God's truth, we see truth. The world, however false its ideas and however shallow some of the people in it, makes true sense. This is because God has made it, and it conforms to something in God's mind. It is a "true" presentation.

But to go back for a moment to the title of this chapter, it is necessary to remind ourselves that this faith that sanctity asks for is not automatic. Faith is planted in our souls at Baptism, but it has to be worked

[20]Cf. John 4:23.

upon by responding to grace. The perfection of faith is *asked for*; it is not mechanically extracted. Nothing is mechanical about sanctity. It all has to be willed, deliberately undertaken, and developed. The grace to be holy is there all right, but its development depends on how generously I respond to it — on how much I *want* to respond to it.

In this whole business of sanctity, the text we need to keep most in mind is the one in which our Lord says that He is "the way and the truth and the life."[21] There is no other way, no other truth, and no other life. It is not as though He merely pointed out the way and then left us to stumble along it: He *is* it. If we live in Christ, we have found the way. Nor does He merely point to some vague, distant, hidden truth, and then leave us to break our brains trying to work it out: He *is* it. If we live in Christ, we have found the truth and our true selves. Nor is the life He offers some sort of supraplanetary, outer-space life: it is the life He lived on earth among men and still lives among us. We are able to share it. He can become our very life. That is exactly what He is to the saints.

[21]John 14:6.

Holiness

∞

So what sanctity asks of us goes deep in, and we need great faith and courage to respond. It is like letting down a bucket into a deep and dark well. The thought may rather scare us, but we must remember that there is living water at the bottom of it. "If any man thirst," says our Lord, "let him come to me and drink."[22] If it is the darkness that frightens us (because the saints certainly do go on and on about the darkness of holiness), we must remember that He is the light of the world. Perseverance is required, because hauling up the bucket is a slow and tiring job, but we must remember that we are not left to our own strength alone. In fact, according to St. Paul, the weaker we are, the more we can count on the strength of God. "Power is made perfect," St. Paul says, "in infirmity."[23] So, trusting in the help of God, we simply go on pulling. Perseverance means being faithful — full of faith. He that perseveres to the end, he shall be sanctified.[24]

[22]John 7:37.
[23]2 Cor. 12:9.
[24]Cf. Matt. 10:22.

Chapter 6

What Holiness Leads To

If faith was the main idea running through the chapter you have just read, hope is the main idea of this one. Hope here is to be thought of not only as looking forward to Heaven, which will be granted us if we do our part in this life, but more especially as having confidence in the power of God to straighten out our muddled lives even now while we are still living. The first meaning of this theological virtue is certainly pointed toward the everlasting happiness that will fulfill the promises of Christ, but there is a nearer meaning of it that looks to God's Providence from day to day. It is this second sort of hope that sanctity develops and brings to perfection.

For instance, the clause "Thy kingdom come" in the Our Father expresses the long-distance hope, whereas the clause "Give us this day our daily bread" expresses the local hope. Sanctity touches both, but one of its more immediate effects is to enlarge the virtue of trust: the conviction that God *is* giving us our daily bread, and will go on doing so. It is a side of hope that is very close to faith, and for this reason it makes the same demands upon us as faith does: perseverance and prayer and the single eye that looks below the surface for the things of God and refuses the worldly view. If "the just man lives by faith,"[25] and if charity is both the "bond"[26] of the just man's perfection and the "urge"[27] that sets him to work upon it, hope is his greatest support. Most of our difficulties and failures come because we too easily lose heart.

Now, hope starts off by knowing that life is going to be difficult. It admits that, without grace, perfection is miles out of reach. It faces the idea of failure. It sees how there are bound to be disappointments and temptations all along the line. But it just goes right on trusting. A person who is strong in this kind of hope looks upon everything that comes along — even mistakes and serious failures — as being a chance not to be missed. Instead of sinking into a mood of despair and self-pity, such a person says simply, "This has turned out wrong,

[25] Hab. 2:4; Rom. 1:17; Gal. 3:11.
[26] Col. 3:14.
[27] Cf. 2 Cor. 5:14.

and everything is in a mess, and I have no idea how it is going to be put right, but I can still count absolutely on the Providence of God."

You can see how, if we are to be saints, we shall need hope at every step. Perhaps the most important stage in his journey toward perfection is the stage when a soul realizes that the whole of life lies in the hollow of God's hand. From that point onward the soul can look at all the happenings that take place as one who looks down at them from a height: he is seeing them from God's angle. So he never lets himself get upset; he is always ready for the next thing; he is never surprised at his own blunders. He refuses to worry about his own point of view because he is far more concerned with God's.

God is the only person who knows how your prayer is getting on, so why fuss? God is the only person who can judge what sort of a character you really have, so why look into yourself and get discouraged and put on an act? God is the only person who can tell how far you have gotten in the journey toward Him, so why try to measure the distance and put in little flags to show that you are making the grade? Leave all that to God — in trust. It is not easy to do this, but then faith and hope are not easy virtues to practice in their perfection, and it is faith and hope that are the surest sign that the soul possesses charity. (But we shall keep charity for the next chapter.)

One of the chief differences between the saints and ourselves is that when things go wrong (and they never go absolutely right for very long), the saints take it for granted that God is treating them lovingly and wisely; we, on the other hand, jump at once to the conclusion that God either does not mind what happens to us or is handing out a punishment. Sanctity always gives God the benefit of the doubt. In fact, it gives Him the benefit of a certainty: He cannot go wrong; He has a plan; He never stops loving.

Remember how our Lord spoke of Himself as the Good Shepherd.[28] Try to see what this *means*. Forget about the pretty pictures of Jesus rescuing sweet little lambs, and just think for a minute what goes on in the mind of a shepherd who is good. Such a shepherd will want the best for his flock *whatever happens*. If he has to lead his sheep over rough ground, it is only so that they may have better grass to feed on; if he steers them away from shrubs they want to nibble, it is only because he

[28]John 10:11-16, 26-28.

knows what plants are bad for them; if he allows them to stay out in the rain, it is only because they will get weak and flabby unless they spend more time out in the open than around a comfortable fire sheltered from the winds.

Go from thinking what is in the mind of a shepherd who is good to imagining what is in the mind of a sheep who is good. Everyone knows that sheep are great at following. The better the sheep, the more ready it is to take the lead of the shepherd. In other words, the good sheep *trusts*. When the shepherd takes an unexpected path, the sheep tags on and does not question the direction. When the shepherd whistles for the sheepdog and sends it to round up the strays, there are no complaints about cruelty and about the horrible barking and about how much nicer the other dog was before this one came along. Good sheep accept all these things as part of the business of being sheep. Still more, they accept them as part of the business of following a shepherd they trust.

You can see from what has been said in this chapter that sanctity leads to courage. A person has to have great courage if he is to turn away from his own ideas

about safety and trust himself to somebody else's —
even if that somebody else is God. But you have to
understand that this courage is not the kind that is
called daring. To be daring may be far more fun, and we
admire the dashing hero when we see him in a film, but
courage is far more pleasing to God. Daring may be no
more than boldness, the exciting instinct that takes
risks, whereas courage is a deliberately built-up state of
mind. The saints are not daredevils, plunging about
because they love danger; they are cool men and women
who go on and on serving God because it is their duty
to do so. This slow kind of courage is sheer virtue, and
is all the more valuable to God because it is so little
noticed by human beings.

The saints are ready enough to take risks when the
occasions come up — such as when they serve lepers, or
expose themselves to persecution and martyrdom for
the sake of spreading the Faith — but this is always
because they take such risks in their stride as being part
of their service of God, and not because they see them
as something glamorous. The saints are ready to become
fools for Christ's sake,[29] but they do not have to be

[29] Cf. 1 Cor. 4:10.

foolhardy. It is not that they want to make a name for themselves — either as heroes or as saints — but that they want to put God's interests first, and they are prepared to go to any lengths to see that these interests are served.

So you can sum up what this chapter has been about by saying that holiness makes straight for the real things of life, for the real virtues, and does not bother about what things look like on the outside. It leads to true wisdom and knowledge, bypassing the wisdom of the world and the knowledge of affairs. It does not look down on learning and education and getting on in the world — quite the opposite: it tries to develop these things by directing them toward truth — but it refuses to let the *lack* of learning, education, or success make any difference. It knows that there are more important things.

It knows also that people have to be knocked about a good deal before they understand much, and that what is called "experience" is mostly a matter of making mistakes and trying to put them right again. For all this you must have hope, confidence in God. "Though he will slay me, yet will I trust in God":[30] this becomes more and more the fighting text of the just man. A holy man (Father Bede Jarrett) once wrote: "Cannot you be grateful for the road though it be rough and uncertain? It does all a road was ever meant to do. It takes you home."

[30]Cf. Job 13:15.

Chapter 7

What Holiness Relies On

∞

The lifeblood of sanctity is, of course, the charity of Christ. He is the vine, and we are the branches;[31] the branches are alive and fruitful for just as long as they receive the life that belongs to the vine. In the same way, personal sanctity is true and fruitful for just as long as it comes from the person of Christ. Try breaking off a twig from a vine and hanging it over your bed. No matter how long you keep it there, you will never see it produce a bunch of grapes. It will gradually shrivel up and die.

So the great thing is to remain one with the vine, letting yourself grow out of it with the strength it gives you. You must take whatever direction the vine wants you to take, and you must not try to show off to the other branches by growing more quickly than the vine means you to. Leave the question of producing fruit to the way things work out: you will not be fruitless if you "abide in

[31] Cf. John 15:5.

the vine."[32] But do not be dismayed when you find that what looks like something becoming a splendid growth, promising a cluster of grapes in the future, is clipped off. The pruning knife is not stunting your growth, but making sure that you grow better, stronger, and healthier. Do not cry out against the knife; it is doing what you cannot do. You cannot become a saint without the Cross.

Now, if the charity of Christ is our source of sanctity, the more we draw from it, the greater will be the gift we can offer to God. Whatever we possess in the way of natural kindness and friendliness must be made to mingle with His divine charity — and so become supernatural. To be nice to people merely because we happen to like them is not enough; we must set our affection higher up the scale and be nice to them for the love of God. This ought not to be too difficult because affection comes from God and can easily be directed back again to Him.

The trouble is that the flow of charity through us to other people, and through them to God, can often be cut clean off. One of Satan's first objectives is to make us put obstacles in the way of what might be called "the

[32] John 15:4.

holy circulation of love." Just as in history one country has tried to keep another country away by building a wall, so we are apt to put up walls between ourselves and other people. Without open warfare, members of the same human race can glare at one another from their own sides of the wall. Once built, these walls are very hard to pull down. Nations that are afraid of other nations build walls. Nations that have a secret they do not want to share build walls. Then everyone becomes deceitful and suspicious, and this is no way to be. But the world is stiff with walls, and there is very little trust, and that is why wars break out.

Although it is not entirely your fault or mine that there is no true peace in the world, and that freedom is a chancy thing that some countries enjoy while others do not, it is your fault and mine that we allow intolerance in our lives. If all of us tried to be helpful instead of wondering how we were going to be double-crossed, we would all get on far better. But because we *expect* to be double-crossed, we lay ourselves open to *be* double-crossed, and this makes us retreat more and more into uncharity and intolerance.

Now, sanctity cannot take root where there are suspicions and the deliberate refusal to see another person's point of view. A readiness to understand — which supposes a readiness to make allowances for what genuinely cannot be understood — is an absolute condition of charity. You cannot raise up a sanctity where there is no foundation of understanding. It goes by other names (such as sympathy, long-suffering, harmony, consideration, patience, compassion), but the many sides of understanding and tolerance amount to only one thing: charity.

You will find to your surprise that charity is just as difficult to practice toward good people as toward bad ones. The saintly can be very irritating. Making allowances for the sinner is so much preached about that when you hear of his failures, you may feel ready to excuse him. His temptations, his upbringing, his background: these things perhaps lessen his guilt and let him off. But do you make enough allowances for the maddening ways, or for the downright failures, of the soul who is trying to be a saint? All are objects of our charity, not just the obvious ones.

The best way to spread your charity so that it covers the people who are working toward God as well as those who are apparently working away from Him, is to realize that each single person has to find his own way of serving God, and that just because it is not your way, you must not find fault with it. On the contrary, you must try to find the good in it. If you were really humble, you would admit that God was probably better served by this other person's slogging along in his way than by your hopping along in your way.

Notice how St. Paul again and again comes back to the idea that there are many vocations but one Spirit working through all of them.[33] And our Lord Himself says that in His Father's house there are many mansions.[34] The Good Shepherd has an endless number of sheep to look after: each one is different, and they bump into one another, and their bleating must infuriate right and left, but all are going in the same direction. The Good Shepherd is drawing them in His way, and the millions of separate sheep are trotting after Him in theirs.

To be tolerant, and to have sympathy for other people's approach to God, which may be very unlike ours, is a mark of true perfection. This is what St. Catherine of Siena says about it: "Such a one does not make himself

[33] Cf. 1 Cor. 12:4-11.
[34] Cf. John 14:2.

a judge of God's servants nor of any other; he congratulates every example and every state of life. He rejoices more in the different kinds of men that he sees than he would in seeing them all walk by the same way, for so he sees the greatness of God made manifest."

It is this variety that makes holiness practical to us as well as beautiful in itself. If all who wanted to be holy had to become monks and nuns, it would narrow our chances a good deal. Instead of this, there are endless patterns of sanctity to choose from. Since sanctity is the life God has given us lived divinely, we can be saints if we are actors or archbishops, stewardesses or mother foundresses. The whole thing depends on the love of God, and if we really love God, it does not seem to matter much what our profession is.

So if charity is the material of holiness, it follows that the nearer we get to becoming saints, the less critical we shall be of others and the more welcoming. We shall want to forgive, we shall want to share, and we shall want to bring others into the circle of God's love. And all this we shall do because we want to please our Lord. In showing charity, we cannot miss. In almost everything else, we can make fools of ourselves by greed and selfishness, but in the matter of charity, we are giving out God Himself. God *is* charity. He does not say of Himself that He is penance or perseverance, or even that He is obedience or humility; He says of Himself that He is charity — and that those who live in charity are living in Him.[35]

"This is my commandment," says our Lord, "that you should love one another as I have loved you."[36] What could be clearer than that? It means that if God loves us with all the love that is in Him, then we must love with all the love that is in us. The only difference is that God's love for us is infinite whereas our love for one another is finite. But you would be surprised how wide that finite love of ours can be stretched: the love of the saints for their fellow human beings was stretched to include all mankind. Charity, if it is really of God, has to be all-embracing.

So when you think of charity, do not think at once of charity bazaars and rummage sales, of collections and subscriptions and fund-raising letters. Instead think first of God's love for every single person in the world, and try to model yourself on that. If you can reach the stage

[35] Cf. 1 John 4:16.
[36] John 15:12.

of loving every single person in the world, you will be only too glad to help in the various works of charity — whether for the hospitals, the missions, the poor, the old, or simply in being kind to people who need to be treated kindly.

Most of us do not have to go far out of our way to find souls to be nice to. Most of us, however, do have to make an effort to be nice to them for the love of God. And that is where sanctity comes in. Sanctity is not choosing which side of charity we want to follow — love of God or love of neighbor — but choosing both and making them into one.

Chapter 8

The Call to Holiness

∞

A thing that is not understood nearly enough is that by rights we all ought to be saints. Such was the original intention in God's mind. Only when Original Sin came along did the plan have to be changed. It was as though man was designed to be tall and straight and handsome, and then by his own fault, and because of a terrible accident resulting from an act of youthful disobedience, he has grown up into a manhood that is stunted and twisted and no longer good to look upon. Now, the encouraging thought that we have to cling to in this is the fact that by God's grace, fallen man can be straightened out almost as good as new — not quite as good as before the Fall, because when our first parents sinned, they lost innocence and what is called "integrity" or "wholeness." But by becoming a member of Christ's body, a baptized Christian gets back to the state of being a possible saint.

Or you can look at it this way: if you have ever stood in front of a lot of distorting mirrors at a fair, you will remember what a relief it was to see yourself at the end of it in an ordinary one. You may not look as perfect as you would like to look, but at least you do not look as terrible as you did in the various distorted reflections. Nor is this all. Once you have gotten away from the monsters that stared at you from the looking glass and showed you what you might have been, you begin to see what you can now become. You can become a reflection of Christ. It is as though our Lord were at your side and saying: "Now that you are gazing into a true looking glass, you know what you are really like. Look hard, and you will see that you have been made in the image and likeness of me. If you work at it, you can become like me in all things. I shall be with you at every step of the way, and will bring out this likeness for you. What you have to do is to trust me completely and not put any obstacles in the way. If you do this, I will take care of the rest."

Does this sound too fanciful? Well, it is not exaggerated when you look at some of the things Scripture actually says. "This is the will of God, your sanctification."[37] "Be you therefore perfect as the heavenly Father

---

[37] 1 Thess. 4:3.

is perfect."[38] These latter words are Christ's, and He never said anything He did not mean. He was telling us, quite simply, to be saints. It is a wonderful thing to realize that you and I are, at this moment, possible saints. The big question is this: what are we going to do about it?

No, it is not enough just to see; we have to *do*. It is not enough just to hear; we have to listen, and then act. This is what St. James has to say about it: "For if a man be a hearer of the word and not a doer, he shall be compared to a man beholding his own face in a glass. He beheld himself and went his way, and presently forgot what manner of man he was."[39] (So you see the idea of a looking glass is nothing new.) By not doing what we feel drawn to do for God, what we know to be what He really wants, we come in the end to forget how it felt to be drawn by God; we forget what it is that He wants.

At first sight St. James's illustration seems exaggerated. How *could* a person study himself in a glass and then not remember what he looked like? But spiritually this is exactly what can happen. People can be shown

[38] Matt. 5:48.
[39] James 1:23-24.

what their souls are capable of, and what they can do for God if they once get themselves started, and then, because they do not follow up this knowledge with its opportunity and invitation, they can drop the whole thing and never give it another thought. It means that the character they could have had has been left in a storeroom, and the character they have now is a weak and unreliable one. If only they had gone on reminding themselves of that likeness they bore to Christ, they would have gone on becoming more and more like Him every day. Each time they looked into the looking glass of what St. James goes on to call "the perfect law of liberty,"[40] they would have seen less of themselves and more of our Lord. And in the end they would have been able to say with St. Paul, "I live, now not I, but Christ lives in me."[41] The glass is reflecting now not me but Christ, who has taken possession of me — who has drawn my character into His own and given me His life to lead.

So you can see how important it is to know as much as possible about the call to sanctity. It is addressed to

[40]James 1:25.
[41]Gal. 2:20.

you personally by God, and you are expected to answer it. Now, I know what you are going to say. You are going to try to get out of it by saying, "Why me?" You are going to say that if He is calling you to be a saint, He must be calling everybody, and if so, why are there so few who answer Him?

The next thing you will say is that since millions of people do not answer the call to sanctity, and yet manage to get along fairly well, why can you not take your place among the millions? Why do you have to be among the few? The millions may not get to Heaven quite so quickly as the few, but at least they will get there (it is to be hoped) in the end. Might it not be a good thing to stick with the millions?

That is the way most people argue, and that is just what St. James and St. Paul — not to mention our Lord and the Holy Spirit — are up against. Human nature can slide out of almost anything when it puts its mind to it. Well then, forget about "most people" for the moment; forget about "human nature" and "the millions." Remember only the link between God and you. It is a link of grace, a personal relationship. And our Lord has said those two things that have already been quoted — "this is the will of God, your sanctification" and "be you therefore perfect as your heavenly Father is perfect" as if they were spoken to nobody else in the world. It is as if they were a private message to you alone.

We know that when anything is the will of God, there must be the grace to fulfill it. The grace is *there;* we can take it or leave it. If He had said, "This is the will of God, your martyrdom," we would know that the grace to fulfill that particular vocation could be counted upon. We would still be left with our free will. We could still run away from martyrdom, although we would be very great fools to do so. God does not call many to martyrdom, but He does call many — in fact all — to perfection. We are very great fools when we run away from perfection. But the sad part of it is that this is what most of us do. It is sad for two reasons: first, because God is not given the praise that the sanctity of His servants could give Him, and second, because these servants of His would be far, far happier if they were holier.

Then there is that second text — about being as perfect as the heavenly Father. I know what you are going to say about this, too. You are going to say, "Anyway, that's *quite* impossible. How can a human being be as perfect as God?" Before you use it as an excuse to put aside all thought of your becoming a saint, you must listen to the explanation of the text. You would be right in thinking that the words cannot be commanding us finite human creatures to be as holy as the infinite divine Creator. But you would be wrong to think that our Lord was either speaking loosely or deliberately made too much of our obligation. What He was saying could be put like this: just as the Father who is infinite is infinitely perfect, so you who are finite must be perfect according the finite powers that are yours. You will never be as perfect as God, but then, you are not meant to be. Your call is to equal God in living up to the perfection of your nature. God has a divine nature; you have a human one. He is perfect as God; you must be perfect as a human being.

One great lesson you are meant to learn from this is that sanctity is not a matter of reaching a particular milestone on the road to God. It is not a case of being an ordinary person until you come to the milestone, and a saint when you have gotten beyond it. It is a case of using your powers as perfectly as you can. There is no fixed milestone. The only thing that is fixed is the destination — God. The pilgrims on the road are all different, all differently equipped for the journey. Some carry great burdens; some carry less. God adjusts these things to each one's strength. God allows the strong pilgrims to be stung by wasps, the weak ones by mosquitoes. What counts is the love that is in each man's heart. So long as your heart, which may perhaps be a small one compared with the heart of another pilgrim, is going out to God as fully as it can, you have nothing to worry about. You may have a heart the size of a thimble, but if it is doing all it can, it is being as perfect as the heart of a pilgrim far more saintly than you who is pounding away with a heart the size of a milk jug.

You should, to finish this chapter, carry away from it two things especially. The first point to have clearly in your mind is that God wants you to be holy, gives you the grace to be holy, and does not listen to your objections about not wanting to be holier than anyone else. How other people answer the call to holiness is not your business. Look for your own answer, and do not make guesses at what others are doing about theirs. And do not wait to respond to God's grace. You must have heard how St. Augustine prayed, "Lord, make me good — but not yet"; he was taking a great risk. You can go on saying "Not yet" for so long that you forget what it was that you prayed for. In the same way, you can go on saying, "I can't bring myself to take it on," for so long that you come in the end to believe it — and then, of course, you cease to feel the urge to take it on. So it has to be *now*; and your attitude has to be this: by God's grace I can do all things in Him who strengthens me.[42]

The other point to remember is that becoming holy is not like graduating. From the outside it may look as though there are honors degrees and passing degrees, but in reality the whole thing depends on the degree of love. Granted that you are giving out charity as generously as you can, you have passed the only test. How so? Because it means that you have *got* charity, and charity is God, and that is sanctity.

[42] Phil. 4:13.

Chapter 9

The Seal of Holiness

∞

You will see now, if you have taken all of this to heart, how sanctity is not to be confused with a readiness to make pious remarks or the knack of being able to kneel bolt upright in church for long periods of time. Sanctity may show itself in a dozen different ways, but then again, it may not show itself outwardly at all. For instance, you may find yourself learning about holiness from people who have not set out to teach it to you, and who have had no idea that you were learning it from them. The goodness of a person often comes out quite naturally and unconsciously, and passes into other people without anything to show for it that you would notice at the time.

So the seal or sign of true sanctity must be looked for in the way a person thinks and judges and loves. How the person acts will follow the working of his mind. Of course, we can never be quite sure about who is trying to be holy and who is merely pretending. Still less can we be sure about how holy a person has managed to

Holiness

become. The best plan is to try to see something of holiness in everyone, and to leave ourselves open to its influence wherever we come across it. True holiness, when we meet it, is not going to be mistaken for anything else, so we need not worry. The mistake lies in trying to see it in ourselves. This mistake leads in turn very often to a still greater mistake, which is to "switch on" acts of holiness.

Saintly deeds that we read about in the lives of the saints are saintly only because they were inspired by charity. The same deeds performed by us, unless inspired by charity, would be sheer vulgarity in exhibiting a counterfeit holiness. A famous sculptor once said that "to carve like the Greeks, you must think as the Greeks thought and believe what the Greeks believed." It is the same in doing the works of sanctity: you must have the mind of the saints before you start acting as they do.

"If that is the case," you may ask, "what is there to go by? If long prayers and hard penances and great labors among the sick and the poor and in the pulpit are not sure signs, how does anyone ever know? How does the Church come to know? There must be *something* that tells us what a real saint is like." The answer to such a question could be put like this. Yes, there are certain marks that tell of true holiness, but they must be seen not as advertisements for sanctity (in the spirit of "Try This and You Will Get Canonized"), but as evidence of God's grace at work in the soul.

So when the Church looks into the life of someone who has been proposed for beatification and canonization, it has to be ensured that during that person's lifetime there was the practice of heroic virtue, and that this was proved over a period of time. Such virtue has had to be expressed faithfully, exactly, and without letting up when the person was not in the mood. The Church says that when any person perseveres in his God-given state of life without rebellion, self-pity, escape, eccentricity, fussiness, vanity, or a desire to attract personal attention, this can only mean that the grace of God is at work in the soul to an extraordinary degree.

Now, notice what the Church does *not* demand as a sign of the person's holiness. There is no talk of ecstasies and self-torture. The Church is not always impressed by exciting things like people going up in the air when they pray, but it is always impressed when it finds that someone has been living an ordinary commonplace life divinely. While at Nazareth, our Lord lived the life of the place divinely, and that is exactly what the saints have been doing ever since.

So you see how the quiet, humble virtues are a more certain proof of holiness than the ones that make head-lines. Two things especially a soul must possess if holi-ness is to be proved, and they are both rather ordinary things: balance and cheerfulness. Balance means not only taking things calmly but also being able to choose between what is important and what is not. Balance is such a good sign because our first parents had it before the Fall, and holiness brings the soul as nearly as possible to that original state. The Fall *unbalanced* man and upset the right order in life. The right order is for the body to obey the spirit and for the spirit to obey God, but Original Sin meant that the body rebelled against the spirit and the spirit rebelled against God. Now, saints, because they live in God and God lives in them, get the order right. So, of course, they are balanced.

That joy is another sign of holiness is also fairly obvious. Not only does God love a cheerful giver, as the Scripture especially tells us,[43] but people love cheerful givers, too — and rightly so. Where there is peace in

[43] 2 Cor. 9:7.

Christ, there is bound to be joy of heart. How could a person who trusted completely in the mercy of God, who looked forward to Heaven, who saw the whole world and all the people in it as coming from the love of God, not be cheerful? So if you want to be holy and give glory to God, try not to be sad. Sadness is no mark of sanctity. Cross-bearing is a mark of sanctity — so long as it is done cheerfully with Christ.

Chapter 10

The Reward of Holiness

If this were a book of instruction instead of spiritual reading, you would be told that among the highest rewards of sanctity, to be enjoyed even in this life, was a better understanding of the gifts of the Holy Spirit. You would be shown how a saint comes to value more and more, and also to practice more and more, the virtues implanted in his soul by Baptism. But it is not much good telling you about this here because you would only think it was a roundabout way of teaching you the catechism. If you take the trouble, however, to look up the list of the Holy Spirit's gifts and fruits, you will see at once that these virtues are worth striving for before you are a saint and also worth possessing more fully as a reward when at last you have reached some sort of state of holiness.

So leaving aside these virtues, the names of which you are afraid you may have to learn by heart, we can divide the subject of this chapter into how sanctity is rewarded first in the present life and then in the next.

Holiness

Since people often imagine that holiness means being weighed down with crosses all the time, and being so at home in our Lord's Passion as not to have room in their lives for even harmless pleasure, it is important to understand how the service of God brings with it a happiness in this world that is beyond anything that is enjoyed by sinners and earthly pleasure-seekers.

This is after all what our Lord Himself has promised. "My peace I give unto you, not as the world gives. . . .[44] My peace no man can take from you."[45] He offers even in this life to His true servants "a more abundant joy"[46] than anything they may be able to find apart from Him. He says we have only to ask and we shall receive, "that your joy may be full."[47] He says that He has come that we may have life.[48] He says that if any man thirsts he must come to Him and drink.[49] He says of those who leave all things and become His close disciples that they

[44]John 14:27.
[45]Cf. John 16:22.
[46]Cf. John 10:10.
[47]John 16:24.
[48]Cf. John 10:10.
[49]Cf. John 7:37.

will receive a hundredfold here on earth — let alone the reward that awaits them in Heaven.[50]

Notice also what our Lord says about the kingdom of Heaven being within us.[51] He means here and now, or the words are pointless. It is comforting to know that we do not have to wait until we die before we can hope for a taste of Heaven. The kingdom of Heaven must lead to happiness, and if this kingdom is within us, we have already gotten what the world is looking for. And since those who are nearest to the kingdom of Heaven are the saints, it is the saints who enjoy most fully the wonder of grace and happiness that is always inside them.

∞

In thinking that sanctity is rewarded in this way, we must avoid the mistake of aiming at holiness for the sake of the happiness it brings with it. Our Lord makes this clear when He says that we must seek first the kingdom of God, and then all these temporal joys will be added to us.[52] It is the same when He speaks about the burden

[50] Cf. Matt. 19:29.
[51] Cf. Luke 17:21.
[52] Cf. Matt. 6:33.

being light and the yoke sweet.[53] Ease and sweetness are not to be aimed at by themselves: they will be earned when we have taken up our Lord's Cross and started following Him.

∞

The trouble is that we never quite believe what our Lord says about these things; and because we do not take Him at His word, we miss a lot of the happiness that might so easily be ours. You remember how our Lord prayed over Jerusalem, and how sad He was that the people who lived there were spoiling their chances of happiness. "If you had known the things that are to your peace," He said, "but you would not."[54] They *could* have known, but they had wasted their opportunity by following after the wrong sort of thing.

We, like the people of Jerusalem, think too much about reward and not enough about the service that merits the reward. We think too much about *getting*. Our Lord, and the saints with Him, think much more about giving.

[53] Cf. Matt. 11:30.
[54] Cf. Luke 19:42; 13:34.

∞

If even in this life holy people stand to get the best of those things that really matter, in the next life they certainly come into their own. We read in Scripture that it has not entered into the mind of man to know what things are stored up in Heaven for the souls who have loved God on earth.[55] We cannot begin to imagine what it will be like to enjoy God with our whole being, and to know that there will never be an end to it. The nearest we can get to the idea of Heaven is to look at our highest happiness here below, and see what is wrong with it.

The fact is that our moments of high happiness — and we can compare lots of such moments if we like — have been moments only. We have never managed to make them last for long. But even apart from never being able to hang on, and knowing at the time that the pleasure is bound to pass, there is always the feeling at the back of our minds that we have room for more. We can look forward without selfishness and greed to something we know we shall enjoy; we can get every ounce of pleasure out of it while it is going on; we can be grateful for it afterward, and not be in the least resentful

[55] Cf. Isa. 64:4; 1 Cor. 2:9.

of the fact that it could not last forever. But all the time, we feel that there must be something else that would just round it off and make it perfect. That "something else" is, of course, the infinity of God's love.

Until we know the infinity of God's love in a way that we can only know when we are united with it in Heaven, we shall always feel that a very important extra is lacking that should be there. It is an odd fact that although we can get tired of pleasure, we can never convince ourselves that we have had enough. In Heaven we shall not long for anything else anymore because we shall be eternally united to God who is *all*. It will not be a question of having "enough" — the happiness of Heaven does not come and fill you up as though you were a sack — but of having an everlasting desire everlastingly granted.

The best thing to do about Heaven is not to try to picture it, but to think of it quite simply as endless love. We all know that the greatest human happinesses are bound up in one way or another with love. Raised to its highest peak, the idea of affection can give you just an inkling of what Heaven is all about. Forget about harps and clouds and pearly gates. Remember what it is like to be fond of someone, and then, remembering also about infinity and eternity, transfer that fondness to God.

Preachers and writers may tell you that reaching Heaven as the reward of your service on earth will be like coming through a door that opens onto a garden of sunshine and exquisite beauty. Perhaps it will be like that; we just do not know. Certainly if it is like that, the door we have come through will shut out all the darkness that lies on the other side. Think of it in this way if it helps you to get there (anything that helps you to get there is worth thinking about), but St. Augustine is probably nearer the mark when he says, "It is not so much that we shall enter into all joy, as that all joy shall enter into us."

Dom Hubert van Zeller

(1905-1984)

Dom Hubert van Zeller was born in 1905 of English parents in Alexandria, Egypt, where his father was in military service during the time when the country was a British protectorate. Van Zeller was educated privately until the age of nine, when he was sent for the remainder of his schooling to the Benedictine Abbey at Downside, England. Upon completing his education at the age of eighteen, he spent a year working at a Liverpool cotton firm before entering the novitiate at Downside in 1924. Unsettled and distracted by his school duties and desiring a more austere way of life, he struggled with his vocation at Downside for many years, even leaving for a brief period in the 1930s to enter the stricter Carthusian monastery at Parkminster.

After his return to Downside Abbey, van Zeller became more involved in giving retreats and writing on spiritual matters. By the time of his death in 1984, he had written scores of books on prayer and spirituality, which won him a devoted readership throughout the

English-speaking world. In addition to being a writer, van Zeller was a prolific and talented sculptor, whose works grace many churches and monasteries in Britain and the United States.

Although a friend of Oxford-educated Catholic writers such as Ronald Knox and Evelyn Waugh, van Zeller once described his own writing about the Faith as an effort to use "the idiom of every day to urge people of every day to embark upon the spirituality of every day." Written with moving depth and simplicity, van Zeller's books should be read by all Christians seeking to pray and to serve with greater fidelity in these difficult days.

Sophia Institute Press®

∞

Sophia Institute is a nonprofit institution that seeks to restore man's knowledge of eternal truth, including man's knowledge of his own nature, his relation to other persons, and his relation to God.

Sophia Institute Press® serves this end in numerous ways. We publish translations of foreign works to make them accessible for the first time to English-speaking readers. We bring back into print books that have been long out of print. And we publish important new books that fulfill the ideals of Sophia Institute. These books afford readers a rich source of the enduring wisdom of mankind.

Sophia Institute Press® makes high-quality books available to the general public by using advanced technology and by soliciting donations to subsidize our general publishing costs.

Your generosity can help us provide the public with editions of works containing the enduring wisdom of the ages. Please send your tax-deductible contribution to the address below.

The members of the Editorial Board of Sophia Institute Press® welcome questions, comments, and suggestions from all our readers.

For your free catalog, call:
Toll-free: 1-800-888-9344

or write:
Sophia Institute Press®
Box 5284
Manchester, NH 03108

*Sophia Institute is a tax-exempt institution
as defined by the Internal Revenue Code,
Section 501(c)(3). Tax I.D. 22-2548708.*